Session Notes

N O T E B O O K

PERSONAL DETAILS

Name : ....

Address : ....

Email : ....

Phone Number : ....

Fax Number : ....

Log Start Date : ....

Log Book Number : ....

ADDITIONAL INFORMATION

Date	Client Name	Contact No	Session No	Page#	Notes

Date	Client Name	Contact No	Session No	Page#	Notes

Date	Client Name	Contact No	Session No	Page#	Notes

Date : _____ Start time : _____ Session No : _____

Client Name : _____ Topic : _____

Session Talking Points :

✔ _____

✔ _____

✔ _____

✔ _____

Key Points from Previous Session :

✔ _____

✔ _____

✔ _____

✔ _____

Notes : _____

Extra Notes :

_____

_____

_____

_____

_____

_____

_____

Client Actions :

✓ _____

✓ _____

✓ _____

Concerns :

✓ _____

✓ _____

✓ _____

Recommendations :

✓ _____

✓ _____

✓ _____

Overall Comments :

_____

_____

_____

Next Session Talking Points :

✓ _____

✓ _____

✓ _____

Next Session Date : _____   End Time : _____

2

Date : _____ Start time : _____ Session No : _____

Client Name : _____ Topic : _____

Session Talking Points :

✔ _____

✔ _____

✔ _____

✔ _____

Key Points from Previous Session :

✔ _____

✔ _____

✔ _____

✔ _____

Notes : _____

_____

_____

_____

_____

_____

_____

_____

_____

_____

_____

_____

_____

_____

_____

_____

_____

_____

_____

_____

_____

_____

_____

Extra Notes :

_____
_____
_____
_____
_____
_____

Client Actions :

✓ _____   ✓ _____
✓ _____   ✓ _____
✓ _____   ✓ _____

Concerns :   Recommendations :

✓ _____   ✓ _____
✓ _____   ✓ _____
✓ _____   ✓ _____

Overall Comments :

_____
_____
_____
_____

Next Session Talking Points :

✓ _____   ✓ _____
✓ _____   ✓ _____
✓ _____   ✓ _____

Next Session Date : _____   End Time : _____

Date : _____ Start time : _____ Session No : _____

Client Name : _____ Topic : _____

Session Talking Points :

- ✓ _____
- ✓ _____
- ✓ _____
- ✓ _____

Key Points from Previous Session :

- ✓ _____
- ✓ _____
- ✓ _____
- ✓ _____

Notes : _____

_____

_____

_____

_____

_____

_____

_____

_____

_____

_____

_____

_____

_____

_____

_____

_____

_____

_____

_____

_____

Extra Notes :

Client Actions :

- ✔
- ✔
- ✔

Concerns :

- ✔
- ✔
- ✔

Recommendations :

- ✔
- ✔
- ✔

Overall Comments :

Next Session Talking Points :

- ✔
- ✔
- ✔

Next Session Date : _____

End Time : _____

Date : _____ Start time : _____ Session No : _____

Client Name : _____ Topic : _____

Session Talking Points :	Key Points from Previous Session :
✔ _____	✔ _____
✔ _____	✔ _____
✔ _____	✔ _____
✔ _____	✔ _____

Notes : _____

Extra Notes :

_____
_____
_____
_____
_____
_____

Client Actions :

✓ _____ ✓ _____
✓ _____ ✓ _____
✓ _____ ✓ _____

Concerns :   Recommendations :

✓ _____ ✓ _____
✓ _____ ✓ _____
✓ _____ ✓ _____

Overall Comments :

_____
_____
_____

Next Session Talking Points :

✓ _____ ✓ _____
✓ _____ ✓ _____
✓ _____ ✓ _____

Next Session Date : _____ End Time : _____

Date : _____ Start time : _____ Session No : _____

Client Name : _____ Topic : _____

Session Talking Points : Key Points from Previous Session :

✔ _____ ✔ _____

✔ _____ ✔ _____

✔ _____ ✔ _____

✔ _____ ✔ _____

Notes :

Extra Notes :

_____
_____
_____
_____
_____
_____
_____

Client Actions :

✓ _____
✓ _____
✓ _____

Concerns :   ## Recommendations :

✓ _____   ✓ _____
✓ _____   ✓ _____
✓ _____   ✓ _____

Overall Comments :

_____
_____
_____

Next Session Talking Points :

✓ _____
✓ _____
✓ _____

Next Session Date : _____   End Time : _____

10

Date : _____ Start time : _____ Session No : _____

Client Name : _____ Topic : _____

Session Talking Points :

✓ _____

✓ _____

✓ _____

✓ _____

Key Points from Previous Session :

✓ _____

✓ _____

✓ _____

✓ _____

Notes : _____

_____

_____

_____

_____

_____

_____

_____

_____

_____

_____

_____

_____

_____

_____

_____

_____

_____

_____

_____

Extra Notes :

_____
_____
_____
_____
_____
_____
_____

Client Actions :

✓ _____   ✓ _____
✓ _____   ✓ _____
✓ _____   ✓ _____

Concerns :   ### Recommendations :

✓ _____   ✓ _____
✓ _____   ✓ _____
✓ _____   ✓ _____

Overall Comments :

_____
_____
_____
_____

Next Session Talking Points :

✓ _____   ✓ _____
✓ _____   ✓ _____
✓ _____   ✓ _____

Next Session Date : _____   End Time : _____

Date : _____ Start time : _____ Session No : _____

Client Name : _____ Topic : _____

Session Talking Points :   Key Points from Previous Session :

✔ _____   ✔ _____

✔ _____   ✔ _____

✔ _____   ✔ _____

✔ _____   ✔ _____

Notes : _____

_____

_____

_____

_____

_____

_____

_____

_____

_____

_____

_____

_____

_____

_____

_____

_____

_____

Extra Notes :

_____
_____
_____
_____
_____
_____
_____

Client Actions :

✓ _____   ✓ _____
✓ _____   ✓ _____
✓ _____   ✓ _____

Concerns :   ## Recommendations :

✓ _____   ✓ _____
✓ _____   ✓ _____
✓ _____   ✓ _____

Overall Comments :

_____
_____
_____
_____

Next Session Talking Points :

✓ _____   ✓ _____
✓ _____   ✓ _____
✓ _____   ✓ _____

Next Session Date : _____   End Time : _____

14

Date : _____ Start time : _____ Session No : _____

Client Name : _____ Topic : _____

Session Talking Points :   Key Points from Previous Session :

✔ _____   ✔ _____

✔ _____   ✔ _____

✔ _____   ✔ _____

✔ _____   ✔ _____

Notes :

Extra Notes :

_____
_____
_____
_____
_____
_____

Client Actions :

✓ _____ ✓ _____
✓ _____ ✓ _____
✓ _____ ✓ _____

Concerns :   Recommendations :

✓ _____ ✓ _____
✓ _____ ✓ _____
✓ _____ ✓ _____

Overall Comments :

_____
_____
_____

Next Session Talking Points :

✓ _____ ✓ _____
✓ _____ ✓ _____
✓ _____ ✓ _____

Next Session Date : _____   End Time : _____

16

Date : _____ Start time : _____ Session No : _____

Client Name : _____ Topic : _____

Session Talking Points :	Key Points from Previous Session :
✔ _____	✔ _____
✔ _____	✔ _____
✔ _____	✔ _____
✔ _____	✔ _____

Notes : _____

Extra Notes :

_____
_____
_____
_____
_____
_____
_____

Client Actions :

- ✓ _____
- ✓ _____
- ✓ _____

Concerns :

- ✓ _____
- ✓ _____
- ✓ _____

Recommendations :

- ✓ _____
- ✓ _____
- ✓ _____

Overall Comments :

_____
_____
_____
_____

Next Session Talking Points :

- ✓ _____
- ✓ _____
- ✓ _____

Next Session Date : _____   End Time : _____

18

Date : _____ Start time : _____ Session No : _____

Client Name : _____ Topic : _____

Session Talking Points :

✔ _____

✔ _____

✔ _____

✔ _____

Key Points from Previous Session :

✔ _____

✔ _____

✔ _____

✔ _____

Notes : _____

_____

_____

_____

_____

_____

_____

_____

_____

_____

_____

_____

_____

_____

_____

_____

_____

_____

_____

_____

_____

Extra Notes :

_____
_____
_____
_____
_____
_____
_____
_____

Client Actions :

✓ _____
✓ _____
✓ _____

Concerns :

✓ _____
✓ _____
✓ _____

Recommendations :

✓ _____
✓ _____
✓ _____

Overall Comments :

_____
_____
_____
_____

Next Session Talking Points :

✓ _____
✓ _____
✓ _____

Next Session Date : _____   End Time : _____

Date : _____ Start time : _____ Session No : _____

Client Name : _____ Topic : _____

Session Talking Points :

✔ _____

✔ _____

✔ _____

✔ _____

Key Points from Previous Session :

✔ _____

✔ _____

✔ _____

✔ _____

Notes :

Extra Notes :

Client Actions :
✓
✓
✓

Concerns :   Recommendations :
✓   ✓
✓   ✓
✓   ✓

Overall Comments :

Next Session Talking Points :
✓
✓
✓

Next Session Date :   End Time :

Date : _____ Start time : _____ Session No : _____

Client Name : _____ Topic : _____

Session Talking Points :

✔ _____

✔ _____

✔ _____

✔ _____

Key Points from Previous Session :

✔ _____

✔ _____

✔ _____

✔ _____

Notes :

_____

_____

_____

_____

_____

_____

_____

_____

_____

_____

_____

_____

_____

_____

_____

_____

_____

_____

_____

_____

_____

_____

_____

_____

Extra Notes :

_____
_____
_____
_____
_____
_____

Client Actions :

✓ _____
✓ _____
✓ _____

Concerns :

✓ _____

Recommendations :

✓ _____
✓ _____
✓ _____

✓ _____
✓ _____
✓ _____

Overall Comments :

_____
_____
_____

Next Session Talking Points :

✓ _____
✓ _____
✓ _____

Next Session Date : _____   End Time : _____

Date : _____ Start time : _____ Session No : _____

Client Name : _____ Topic : _____

Session Talking Points :   Key Points from Previous Session :

✓ _____   ✓ _____

✓ _____   ✓ _____

✓ _____   ✓ _____

✓ _____   ✓ _____

Notes : _____

Extra Notes :

_____
_____
_____
_____
_____
_____

Client Actions :

✔ _____
✔ _____
✔ _____

Concerns :

✔ _____

Recommendations :

✔ _____
✔ _____
✔ _____

Overall Comments :

_____
_____
_____
_____

Next Session Talking Points :

✔ _____
✔ _____
✔ _____

Next Session Date : _____   End Time : _____

26

Date : _____ Start time : _____ Session No : _____

Client Name : _____ Topic : _____

Session Talking Points : Key Points from Previous Session :

✔ _____ ✔ _____

✔ _____ ✔ _____

✔ _____ ✔ _____

✔ _____ ✔ _____

Notes : _____

Extra Notes :

_____
_____
_____
_____
_____
_____

Client Actions :

✓ _____
✓ _____
✓ _____

Concerns :

✓ _____
✓ _____
✓ _____

Recommendations :

✓ _____
✓ _____
✓ _____

Overall Comments :

_____
_____
_____

Next Session Talking Points :

✓ _____
✓ _____
✓ _____

Next Session Date : _____   End Time : _____

Date : _____ Start time : _____ Session No : _____

Client Name : _____ Topic : _____

Session Talking Points :   Key Points from Previous Session :

✔ _____ ✔ _____

✔ _____ ✔ _____

✔ _____ ✔ _____

✔ _____ ✔ _____

Notes :

Extra Notes :

_____
_____
_____
_____
_____
_____
_____

Client Actions :

✔ _____
✔ _____
✔ _____

Concerns :

✔ _____
✔ _____
✔ _____

Recommendations :

✔ _____
✔ _____
✔ _____

Overall Comments :

_____
_____
_____

Next Session Talking Points :

✔ _____
✔ _____
✔ _____

Next Session Date : _____   End Time : _____

30

Date : _____ Start time : _____ Session No : _____

Client Name : _____ Topic : _____

Session Talking Points :

✔ _____

✔ _____

✔ _____

✔ _____

Key Points from Previous Session :

✔ _____

✔ _____

✔ _____

✔ _____

Notes : _____

Extra Notes :

_____
_____
_____
_____
_____
_____
_____

Client Actions :

✓ _____   ✓ _____
✓ _____   ✓ _____
✓ _____   ✓ _____

Concerns :   ## Recommendations :

✓ _____   ✓ _____
✓ _____   ✓ _____
✓ _____   ✓ _____

Overall Comments :

_____
_____
_____

Next Session Talking Points :

✓ _____   ✓ _____
✓ _____   ✓ _____
✓ _____   ✓ _____

Next Session Date : _____   End Time : _____

Date : _____ Start time : _____ Session No : _____

Client Name : _____ Topic : _____

Session Talking Points :

✔ _____

✔ _____

✔ _____

✔ _____

Key Points from Previous Session :

✔ _____

✔ _____

✔ _____

✔ _____

Notes : _____

Extra Notes :

_____
_____
_____
_____
_____
_____

Client Actions :

✓ _____
✓ _____
✓ _____

Concerns :

Recommendations :

✓ _____
✓ _____
✓ _____

✓ _____
✓ _____
✓ _____

Overall Comments :

_____
_____
_____

Next Session Talking Points :

✓ _____
✓ _____
✓ _____

Next Session Date : _____   End Time : _____

Date : _____ Start time : _____ Session No : _____

Client Name : _____ Topic : _____

Session Talking Points :

- ✔ _____
- ✔ _____
- ✔ _____
- ✔ _____

Key Points from Previous Session :

- ✔ _____
- ✔ _____
- ✔ _____
- ✔ _____

Notes : _____

_____

_____

_____

_____

_____

_____

_____

_____

_____

_____

_____

_____

_____

_____

_____

_____

_____

_____

_____

_____

Extra Notes :

_____
_____
_____
_____
_____
_____

Client Actions :

✓ _____   ✓ _____
✓ _____   ✓ _____
✓ _____   ✓ _____

Concerns :   Recommendations :

✓ _____   ✓ _____
✓ _____   ✓ _____
✓ _____   ✓ _____

Overall Comments :

_____
_____
_____

Next Session Talking Points :

✓ _____   ✓ _____
✓ _____   ✓ _____
✓ _____   ✓ _____

Next Session Date : _____   End Time : _____

36

Date : _____ Start time : _____ Session No : _____

Client Name : _____ Topic : _____

Session Talking Points :

✔ _____
✔ _____
✔ _____
✔ _____

Key Points from Previous Session :

✔ _____
✔ _____
✔ _____
✔ _____

Notes : _____

_____
_____
_____
_____
_____
_____
_____
_____
_____
_____
_____
_____
_____
_____
_____
_____
_____
_____
_____
_____
_____
_____

Extra Notes :

_____
_____
_____
_____
_____
_____
_____
_____

Client Actions :

✔ _____
✔ _____
✔ _____
✔ _____
✔ _____
✔ _____

Concerns :

Recommendations :

✔ _____
✔ _____
✔ _____

Overall Comments :

_____
_____
_____
_____

Next Session Talking Points :

✔ _____
✔ _____
✔ _____
✔ _____
✔ _____
✔ _____

Next Session Date : _____   End Time : _____

Date : _____ Start time : _____ Session No : _____

Client Name : _____ Topic : _____

Session Talking Points :

✔ _____

✔ _____

✔ _____

✔ _____

Key Points from Previous Session :

✔ _____

✔ _____

✔ _____

✔ _____

Notes : _____

_____

_____

_____

_____

_____

_____

_____

_____

_____

_____

_____

_____

_____

_____

_____

_____

_____

_____

Extra Notes :

_____
_____
_____
_____
_____
_____
_____

Client Actions :

✓ _____ ✓ _____
✓ _____ ✓ _____
✓ _____ ✓ _____

Concerns :   Recommendations :

✓ _____ ✓ _____
✓ _____ ✓ _____
✓ _____ ✓ _____

Overall Comments :

_____
_____
_____
_____

Next Session Talking Points :

✓ _____ ✓ _____
✓ _____ ✓ _____
✓ _____ ✓ _____

Next Session Date : _____   End Time : _____

Date : _____ Start time : _____ Session No : _____

Client Name : _____ Topic : _____

Session Talking Points :

✔ _____

✔ _____

✔ _____

✔ _____

Key Points from Previous Session :

✔ _____

✔ _____

✔ _____

✔ _____

Notes : _____

_____

_____

_____

_____

_____

_____

_____

_____

_____

_____

_____

_____

_____

_____

_____

_____

_____

_____

_____

Extra Notes :

Client Actions :
✔
✔
✔

Concerns :
✔
✔
✔

Recommendations :
✔
✔
✔

Overall Comments :

Next Session Talking Points :
✔
✔
✔

Next Session Date : _____   End Time : _____

Date : _____ Start time : _____ Session No : _____

Client Name : _____ Topic : _____

Session Talking Points :   Key Points from Previous Session :

✔ _____   ✔ _____

✔ _____   ✔ _____

✔ _____   ✔ _____

✔ _____   ✔ _____

Notes : _____

Extra Notes :

_____
_____
_____
_____
_____
_____

Client Actions :

✔ _____
✔ _____
✔ _____

Concerns :   ## Recommendations :

✔ _____
✔ _____
✔ _____

Overall Comments :

_____
_____
_____

Next Session Talking Points :

✔ _____
✔ _____
✔ _____

Next Session Date : _____   End Time : _____

Date : _____ Start time : _____ Session No : _____

Client Name : _____ Topic : _____

Session Talking Points :   Key Points from Previous Session :

✔ _____   ✔ _____

✔ _____   ✔ _____

✔ _____   ✔ _____

✔ _____   ✔ _____

Notes : _____

_____

_____

_____

_____

_____

_____

_____

_____

_____

_____

_____

_____

_____

_____

_____

_____

_____

_____

_____

Extra Notes :

Client Actions :

✔
✔
✔

Concerns :

✔
✔
✔

Recommendations :

✔
✔
✔

Overall Comments :

Next Session Talking Points :

✔
✔
✔

Next Session Date : _____   End Time : _____

Date : _____ Start time : _____ Session No : _____

Client Name : _____ Topic : _____

Session Talking Points :

✔ _____

✔ _____

✔ _____

✔ _____

Key Points from Previous Session :

✔ _____

✔ _____

✔ _____

✔ _____

Notes : _____

_____

_____

_____

_____

_____

_____

_____

_____

_____

_____

_____

_____

_____

_____

_____

_____

_____

_____

_____

_____

_____

_____

_____

_____

_____

Extra Notes :

_____
_____
_____
_____
_____
_____
_____

Client Actions :

✓ _____
✓   ✓ _____
✓   ✓ _____
✓   ✓ _____

Concerns :   Recommendations :

✓ _____
✓   ✓ _____
✓   ✓ _____
✓   ✓ _____

Overall Comments :

_____
_____
_____

Next Session Talking Points :

✓ _____
✓   ✓ _____
✓   ✓ _____
✓   ✓ _____

Next Session Date : _____   End Time : _____

Date : _____ Start time : _____ Session No : _____

Client Name : _____ Topic : _____

Session Talking Points :

✔ _____

✔ _____

✔ _____

✔ _____

Key Points from Previous Session :

✔ _____

✔ _____

✔ _____

✔ _____

Notes : _____

_____

_____

_____

_____

_____

_____

_____

_____

_____

_____

_____

_____

_____

_____

_____

_____

_____

_____

Extra Notes :

Client Actions :

✓
✓
✓

Concerns :

Recommendations :

✓
✓
✓

✓
✓
✓

Overall Comments :

Next Session Talking Points :

✓
✓
✓

Next Session Date : _____ End Time : _____

Date : _____ Start time : _____ Session No : _____

Client Name : _____ Topic : _____

Session Talking Points :

✔ _____

✔ _____

✔ _____

✔ _____

Key Points from Previous Session :

✔ _____

✔ _____

✔ _____

✔ _____

Notes : _____

_____

_____

_____

_____

_____

_____

_____

_____

_____

_____

_____

_____

_____

_____

_____

_____

_____

_____

_____

_____

_____

Extra Notes :

Client Actions :

✓
✓
✓

Concerns :

✓
✓
✓

Recommendations :

✓
✓
✓

Overall Comments :

Next Session Talking Points :

✓
✓
✓

Next Session Date : _____ End Time : _____

Date : _____   Start time : _____   Session No : _____

Client Name : _____   Topic : _____

Session Talking Points :   Key Points from Previous Session :

✔ _____   ✔ _____

✔ _____   ✔ _____

✔ _____   ✔ _____

✔ _____   ✔ _____

Notes : _____

Extra Notes :

_____
_____
_____
_____
_____
_____
_____

Client Actions :

✓ _____
✓ _____
✓ _____

Concerns :

✓ _____
✓ _____
✓ _____

Recommendations :

✓ _____
✓ _____
✓ _____

Overall Comments :

_____
_____
_____

Next Session Talking Points :

✓ _____
✓ _____
✓ _____

Next Session Date : _____   End Time : _____

Date : _____ Start time : _____ Session No : _____

Client Name : _____ Topic : _____

Session Talking Points :

✔ _____

✔ _____

✔ _____

✔ _____

Key Points from Previous Session :

✔ _____

✔ _____

✔ _____

✔ _____

Notes :

Extra Notes :

_____
_____
_____
_____
_____
_____
_____

Client Actions :

✓_____   ✓_____
✓_____   ✓_____
✓_____   ✓_____

Concerns :   ## Recommendations :

✓_____   ✓_____
✓_____   ✓_____
✓_____   ✓_____

Overall Comments :

_____
_____
_____

Next Session Talking Points :

✓_____   ✓_____
✓_____   ✓_____
✓_____   ✓_____

Next Session Date : _____   End Time : _____

Date : _____ Start time : _____ Session No : _____

Client Name : _____ Topic : _____

<table>
<tr><td>Session Talking Points :</td><td>Key Points from Previous Session :</td></tr>
<tr><td>✔ _____</td><td>✔ _____</td></tr>
<tr><td>✔ _____</td><td>✔ _____</td></tr>
<tr><td>✔ _____</td><td>✔ _____</td></tr>
<tr><td>✔ _____</td><td>✔ _____</td></tr>
</table>

Notes :

_____

_____

_____

_____

_____

_____

_____

_____

_____

_____

_____

_____

_____

_____

_____

_____

_____

_____

_____

Extra Notes :

_____
_____
_____
_____
_____
_____
_____

Client Actions :

✓
- ✓ _____
✓
- ✓ _____
✓
- ✓ _____

Concerns :

✓
- ✓ _____
✓
- ✓ _____
✓
- ✓ _____

Recommendations :

- ✓ _____
- ✓ _____
- ✓ _____

Overall Comments :

_____
_____
_____

Next Session Talking Points :

✓
- ✓ _____
✓
- ✓ _____
✓
- ✓ _____

Next Session Date : _____   End Time : _____

58

Date : _____ Start time : _____ Session No : _____

Client Name : _____ Topic : _____

Session Talking Points :

✔ _____

✔ _____

✔ _____

✔ _____

Key Points from Previous Session :

✔ _____

✔ _____

✔ _____

✔ _____

Notes :

Extra Notes :

Client Actions :
✓
✓
✓

Concerns :
✓
✓
✓

Recommendations :
✓
✓
✓

Overall Comments :

Next Session Talking Points :
✓
✓
✓

Next Session Date : _____   End Time : _____

Date : _____ Start time : _____ Session No : _____

Client Name : _____ Topic : _____

Session Talking Points :

✓ _____
✓ _____
✓ _____
✓ _____

Key Points from Previous Session :

✓ _____
✓ _____
✓ _____
✓ _____

Notes :

_____
_____
_____
_____
_____
_____
_____
_____
_____
_____
_____
_____
_____
_____
_____
_____
_____
_____
_____
_____

Extra Notes :

_____
_____
_____
_____
_____
_____
_____

Client Actions :

✔ _____
✔ _____
✔ _____

Concerns :

✔ _____
✔ _____
✔ _____

Recommendations :

✔ _____
✔ _____
✔ _____

Overall Comments :

_____
_____
_____
_____

Next Session Talking Points :

✔ _____
✔ _____
✔ _____

Next Session Date : _____   End Time : _____

Date : _____ Start time : _____ Session No : _____

Client Name : _____ Topic : _____

Session Talking Points :

- ✔ _____
- ✔ _____
- ✔ _____
- ✔ _____

Key Points from Previous Session :

- ✔ _____
- ✔ _____
- ✔ _____
- ✔ _____

Notes : _____

_____

_____

_____

_____

_____

_____

_____

_____

_____

_____

_____

_____

_____

_____

_____

_____

_____

_____

_____

_____

_____

Extra Notes :

_____
_____
_____
_____
_____
_____
_____
_____

Client Actions :

✔ _____
✔ _____
✔ _____

    ✔ _____
    ✔ _____
    ✔ _____

Concerns :   Recommendations :

✔ _____   ✔ _____
✔ _____   ✔ _____
✔ _____   ✔ _____

Overall Comments :

_____
_____
_____
_____

Next Session Talking Points :

✔ _____
✔ _____
✔ _____

    ✔ _____
    ✔ _____
    ✔ _____

Next Session Date : _____ End Time : _____

Date : _____ Start time : _____ Session No : _____

Client Name : _____ Topic : _____

Session Talking Points :

✔ _____
✔ _____
✔ _____
✔ _____

Key Points from Previous Session :

✔ _____
✔ _____
✔ _____
✔ _____

Notes : _____

_____

_____

_____

_____

_____

_____

_____

_____

_____

_____

_____

_____

_____

_____

_____

_____

_____

_____

_____

_____

_____

Extra Notes :

_____
_____
_____
_____
_____
_____

Client Actions :

✓ _____   ✓ _____
✓ _____   ✓ _____
✓ _____   ✓ _____

Concerns :   Recommendations :

✓ _____   ✓ _____
✓ _____   ✓ _____
✓ _____   ✓ _____

Overall Comments :

_____
_____
_____

Next Session Talking Points :

✓ _____   ✓ _____
✓ _____   ✓ _____
✓ _____   ✓ _____

Next Session Date : _____   End Time : _____

66

Date : _____ Start time : _____ Session No : _____

Client Name : _____ Topic : _____

Session Talking Points :

✔ _____

✔ _____

✔ _____

✔ _____

Key Points from Previous Session :

✔ _____

✔ _____

✔ _____

✔ _____

Notes : _____

Extra Notes :

_____
_____
_____
_____
_____
_____

Client Actions :

✓_____   ✓_____
✓_____   ✓_____
✓_____   ✓_____

Concerns :   ## Recommendations :

✓_____   ✓_____
✓_____   ✓_____
✓_____   ✓_____

Overall Comments :

_____
_____
_____
_____

Next Session Talking Points :

✓_____   ✓_____
✓_____   ✓_____
✓_____   ✓_____

Next Session Date : _____   End Time : _____

68

Date : _____ Start time : _____ Session No : _____

Client Name : _____ Topic : _____

_____

| Session Talking Points : | Key Points from Previous Session : |

✔ _____   ✔ _____

✔ _____   ✔ _____

✔ _____   ✔ _____

✔ _____   ✔ _____

Notes : _____

_____
_____
_____
_____
_____
_____
_____
_____
_____
_____
_____
_____
_____
_____
_____
_____
_____
_____
_____
_____

Extra Notes :

Client Actions :

✔
✔
✔

Concerns :

✔
✔
✔

Recommendations :

✔
✔
✔

Overall Comments :

Next Session Talking Points :

✔
✔
✔

Next Session Date : _____   End Time : _____

Date : _____ Start time : _____ Session No : _____

Client Name : _____ Topic : _____

_____

Session Talking Points :   Key Points from Previous Session :

✔ _____   ✔ _____

✔ _____   ✔ _____

✔ _____   ✔ _____

✔ _____   ✔ _____

Notes : _____

_____

_____

_____

_____

_____

_____

_____

_____

_____

_____

_____

_____

_____

_____

_____

_____

_____

_____

_____

_____

_____

_____

Extra Notes :

_____
_____
_____
_____
_____
_____
_____

Client Actions :

✓ _____   ✓ _____
✓ _____   ✓ _____
✓ _____   ✓ _____

Concerns :   ## Recommendations :

✓ _____   ✓ _____
✓ _____   ✓ _____
✓ _____   ✓ _____

Overall Comments :

_____
_____
_____

Next Session Talking Points :

✓ _____   ✓ _____
✓ _____   ✓ _____
✓ _____   ✓ _____

Next Session Date : _____   End Time : _____

Date : _____ Start time : _____ Session No : _____

Client Name : _____ Topic : _____

Session Talking Points :

✔ _____

✔ _____

✔ _____

✔ _____

Key Points from Previous Session :

✔ _____

✔ _____

✔ _____

✔ _____

Notes : _____

_____

_____

_____

_____

_____

_____

_____

_____

_____

_____

_____

_____

_____

_____

_____

_____

_____

Extra Notes :

_____
_____
_____
_____
_____
_____
_____

Client Actions :

✔ _____
✔ _____
✔ _____

Concerns :

Recommendations :

✔ _____
✔ _____
✔ _____

Overall Comments :

_____
_____
_____

Next Session Talking Points :

✔ _____
✔ _____
✔ _____

Next Session Date : _____   End Time : _____

74

Date : _____ Start time : _____ Session No : _____

Client Name : _____ Topic : _____

_____

Session Talking Points :   Key Points from Previous Session :

✔ _____   ✔ _____

✔ _____   ✔ _____

✔ _____   ✔ _____

✔ _____   ✔ _____

Notes : _____

_____

_____

_____

_____

_____

_____

_____

_____

_____

_____

_____

_____

_____

_____

_____

_____

_____

_____

_____

_____

_____

_____

Extra Notes :

_____
_____
_____
_____
_____
_____
_____

Client Actions :

✓ _____
✓ _____
✓ _____

Concerns :

✓ _____
✓ _____
✓ _____

Recommendations :

✓ _____
✓ _____
✓ _____

Overall Comments :

_____
_____
_____
_____

Next Session Talking Points :

✓ _____
✓ _____
✓ _____

Next Session Date : _____   End Time : _____

Date : _____ Start time : _____ Session No : _____

Client Name : _____ Topic : _____

Session Talking Points :	Key Points from Previous Session :
✓ _____	✓ _____
✓ _____	✓ _____
✓ _____	✓ _____
✓ _____	✓ _____

Notes : _____

Extra Notes :

_____
_____
_____
_____
_____
_____
_____

Client Actions :

✓ _____

✓ _____

✓ _____

Concerns :

✓ _____

✓ _____

✓ _____

Recommendations :

✓ _____

✓ _____

✓ _____

Overall Comments :

_____
_____
_____
_____

Next Session Talking Points :

✓ _____

✓ _____

✓ _____

Next Session Date : _____   End Time : _____

Date : _____ Start time : _____ Session No : _____

Client Name : _____ Topic : _____

Session Talking Points :

✔ _____

✔ _____

✔ _____

✔ _____

Key Points from Previous Session :

✔ _____

✔ _____

✔ _____

✔ _____

Notes : _____

Extra Notes :

_____
_____
_____
_____
_____
_____
_____

Client Actions :

✓ _____
✓ _____
✓ _____

Concerns :

✓ _____
✓ _____
✓ _____

Recommendations :

✓ _____
✓ _____
✓ _____

Overall Comments :

_____
_____
_____
_____

Next Session Talking Points :

✓ _____
✓ _____
✓ _____

Next Session Date : _____   End Time : _____

Date :   Start time :   Session No :

Client Name :   Topic :

Session Talking Points :   Key Points from Previous Session :

✔   ✔

✔   ✔

✔   ✔

✔   ✔

Notes :

Extra Notes :

Client Actions :
✓
✓
✓

✓
✓
✓

Concerns :

Recommendations :

✓
✓
✓

✓
✓
✓

Overall Comments :

Next Session Talking Points :
✓
✓
✓

✓
✓
✓

Next Session Date : _____   End Time : _____

Date : _____ Start time : _____ Session No : _____

Client Name : _____ Topic : _____

Session Talking Points :

✔ _____

✔ _____

✔ _____

✔ _____

Key Points from Previous Session :

✔ _____

✔ _____

✔ _____

✔ _____

Notes :

Extra Notes :

_____
_____
_____
_____
_____
_____
_____

Client Actions :

✓_____   ✓_____
✓_____   ✓_____
✓_____   ✓_____

Concerns :   Recommendations :

✓_____   ✓_____
✓_____   ✓_____
✓_____   ✓_____

Overall Comments :

_____
_____
_____
_____

Next Session Talking Points :

✓_____   ✓_____
✓_____   ✓_____
✓_____   ✓_____

Next Session Date : _____   End Time : _____

84

Date : _____ Start time : _____ Session No : _____

Client Name : _____ Topic : _____

Session Talking Points :

✔ _____

✔ _____

✔ _____

✔ _____

Key Points from Previous Session :

✔ _____

✔ _____

✔ _____

✔ _____

Notes :

Extra Notes :

Client Actions :
- ✔
- ✔
- ✔

Concerns :
- ✔
- ✔
- ✔

Recommendations :
- ✔
- ✔
- ✔

Overall Comments :

Next Session Talking Points :
- ✔
- ✔
- ✔

Next Session Date :   End Time :

Date : _____ Start time : _____ Session No : _____

Client Name : _____ Topic : _____

Session Talking Points :   Key Points from Previous Session :

✔ _____   ✔ _____

✔ _____   ✔ _____

✔ _____   ✔ _____

✔ _____   ✔ _____

Notes : _____

_____

_____

_____

_____

_____

_____

_____

_____

_____

_____

_____

_____

_____

_____

_____

_____

_____

_____

_____

_____

_____

Extra Notes :

_____
_____
_____
_____
_____
_____
_____

Client Actions :

✓ _____ ✓ _____
✓ _____ ✓ _____
✓ _____ ✓ _____

Concerns :   Recommendations :

✓ _____ ✓ _____
✓ _____ ✓ _____
✓ _____ ✓ _____

Overall Comments :

_____
_____
_____
_____

Next Session Talking Points :

✓ _____ ✓ _____
✓ _____ ✓ _____
✓ _____ ✓ _____

Next Session Date : _____   End Time : _____

Date :   Start time :   Session No :

Client Name :   Topic :

Session Talking Points :   Key Points from Previous Session :

✔ _____   ✔ _____

✔ _____   ✔ _____

✔ _____   ✔ _____

✔ _____   ✔ _____

Notes :

Extra Notes :

Client Actions :

✓
✓
✓

✓
✓
✓

Concerns :

✓
✓
✓

Recommendations :

✓
✓
✓

Overall Comments :

Next Session Talking Points :

✓
✓
✓

✓
✓
✓

Next Session Date : _____   End Time : _____

Date : _____ Start time : _____ Session No : _____

Client Name : _____ Topic : _____

Session Talking Points :   Key Points from Previous Session :

✔ _____   ✔ _____

✔ _____   ✔ _____

✔ _____   ✔ _____

✔ _____   ✔ _____

Notes : _____

_____

_____

_____

_____

_____

_____

_____

_____

_____

_____

_____

_____

_____

_____

_____

_____

_____

_____

_____

_____

_____

_____

Extra Notes :

_____
_____
_____
_____
_____
_____

Client Actions :

✓ _____ ✓ _____
✓ _____ ✓ _____
✓ _____ ✓ _____

Concerns :   Recommendations :

✓ _____ ✓ _____
✓ _____ ✓ _____
✓ _____ ✓ _____

Overall Comments :

_____
_____
_____
_____

Next Session Talking Points :

✓ _____
✓ _____
✓ _____

Next Session Date : _____   End Time : _____

92

Date : _____   Start time : _____   Session No : _____

Client Name : _____   Topic : _____

Session Talking Points :	Key Points from Previous Session :
✓ _____	✓ _____
✓ _____	✓ _____
✓ _____	✓ _____
✓ _____	✓ _____

Notes : _____

_____

_____

_____

_____

_____

_____

_____

_____

_____

_____

_____

_____

_____

_____

_____

_____

_____

_____

Extra Notes :

Client Actions :
✓
✓
✓

Concerns :
✓
✓
✓

Recommendations :
✓
✓
✓

Overall Comments :

Next Session Talking Points :
✓
✓
✓

Next Session Date : _____   End Time : _____

Date : _____ Start time : _____ Session No : _____

Client Name : _____ Topic : _____

Session Talking Points :   Key Points from Previous Session :

✔ _____   ✔ _____

✔ _____   ✔ _____

✔ _____   ✔ _____

✔ _____   ✔ _____

Notes :

Extra Notes :

Client Actions :
✓
✓
✓

Concerns :   Recommendations :
✓
✓
✓

Overall Comments :

Next Session Talking Points :
✓
✓
✓

Next Session Date :   End Time :

Date : _____ Start time : _____ Session No : _____

Client Name : _____ Topic : _____

Session Talking Points :   Key Points from Previous Session :

✔ _____   ✔ _____

✔ _____   ✔ _____

✔ _____   ✔ _____

✔ _____   ✔ _____

Notes : _____

Extra Notes :

_____

_____

_____

_____

_____

_____

Client Actions :

✓ _____

✓ _____

✓ _____

✓ _____

✓ _____

✓ _____

Concerns :

Recommendations :

✓ _____

✓ _____

✓ _____

✓ _____

✓ _____

✓ _____

Overall Comments :

_____

_____

_____

Next Session Talking Points :

✓ _____

✓ _____

✓ _____

✓ _____

✓ _____

✓ _____

Next Session Date : _____   End Time : _____

Date : _____ Start time : _____ Session No : _____

Client Name : _____ Topic : _____

Session Talking Points :

- ✔ _____
- ✔ _____
- ✔ _____
- ✔ _____

Key Points from Previous Session :

- ✔ _____
- ✔ _____
- ✔ _____
- ✔ _____

Notes : _____

_____

_____

_____

_____

_____

_____

_____

_____

_____

_____

_____

_____

_____

_____

_____

_____

_____

_____

_____

_____

_____

_____

Extra Notes :

_____
_____
_____
_____
_____
_____

Client Actions :

✓_____   ✓_____
✓_____   ✓_____
✓_____   ✓_____

Concerns :   Recommendations :

✓_____   ✓_____
✓_____   ✓_____
✓_____   ✓_____

Overall Comments :

_____
_____
_____

Next Session Talking Points :

✓_____   ✓_____
✓_____   ✓_____
✓_____   ✓_____

Next Session Date :_____   End Time :_____

Date : _____   Start time : _____   Session No : _____

Client Name : _____   Topic : _____

Session Talking Points :	Key Points from Previous Session :
✔ _____	✔ _____
✔ _____	✔ _____
✔ _____	✔ _____
✔ _____	✔ _____

Notes : _____

_____

_____

_____

_____

_____

_____

_____

_____

_____

_____

_____

_____

_____

_____

_____

_____

_____

_____

Extra Notes :

_____
_____
_____
_____
_____
_____
_____

Client Actions :

✓ _____
✓ _____
✓ _____

Concerns :

✓ _____
✓ _____
✓ _____

Recommendations :

✓ _____
✓ _____
✓ _____

Overall Comments :

_____
_____
_____

Next Session Talking Points :

✓ _____
✓ _____
✓ _____

Next Session Date : _____   End Time : _____

Date : _____ Start time : _____ Session No : _____

Client Name : _____ Topic : _____

Session Talking Points :

✔ _____

✔ _____

✔ _____

✔ _____

Key Points from Previous Session :

✔ _____

✔ _____

✔ _____

✔ _____

Notes : _____

_____

_____

_____

_____

_____

_____

_____

_____

_____

_____

_____

_____

_____

_____

_____

_____

_____

_____

_____

_____

_____

Extra Notes :

Client Actions :
- ✓
- ✓
- ✓

Concerns :
- ✓
- ✓
- ✓

Recommendations :
- ✓
- ✓
- ✓

Overall Comments :

Next Session Talking Points :
- ✓
- ✓
- ✓

Next Session Date : _____   End Time : _____

Date : _____ Start time : _____ Session No : _____

Client Name : _____ Topic : _____

Session Talking Points : Key Points from Previous Session :

✔ _____ ✔ _____

✔ _____ ✔ _____

✔ _____ ✔ _____

✔ _____ ✔ _____

Notes : _____

Extra Notes :

Client Actions :

✔
✔
✔

Concerns :

✔
✔
✔

Recommendations :

✔
✔
✔

Overall Comments :

Next Session Talking Points :

✔
✔
✔

Next Session Date :   End Time :

Date : _____ Start time : _____ Session No : _____

Client Name : _____ Topic : _____

_____

Session Talking Points :

✔ _____

✔ _____

✔ _____

✔ _____

Key Points from Previous Session :

✔ _____

✔ _____

✔ _____

✔ _____

Notes : _____

_____

_____

_____

_____

_____

_____

_____

_____

_____

_____

_____

_____

_____

_____

_____

_____

_____

_____

_____

_____

Extra Notes :

_____

Client Actions :

✓ _____
✓ _____
✓ _____

Concerns :

✓ _____
✓ _____
✓ _____

Recommendations :

✓ _____
✓ _____
✓ _____

Overall Comments :

_____

Next Session Talking Points :

✓ _____
✓ _____
✓ _____

Next Session Date : _____   End Time : _____

Date : _____ Start time : _____ Session No : _____

Client Name : _____ Topic : _____

Session Talking Points :

✓ _____

✓ _____

✓ _____

✓ _____

Key Points from Previous Session :

✓ _____

✓ _____

✓ _____

✓ _____

Notes : _____

_____

_____

_____

_____

_____

_____

_____

_____

_____

_____

_____

_____

_____

_____

_____

_____

_____

Extra Notes :

Client Actions :

✔
✔
✔

Concerns :

✔
✔
✔

Recommendations :

✔
✔
✔

Overall Comments :

Next Session Talking Points :

✔
✔
✔

Next Session Date : _____   End Time : _____

Date : _____ Start time : _____ Session No : _____

Client Name : _____ Topic : _____

Session Talking Points :   Key Points from Previous Session :

✔ _____   ✔ _____

✔ _____   ✔ _____

✔ _____   ✔ _____

✔ _____   ✔ _____

Notes :

Extra Notes :

_____
_____
_____
_____
_____
_____
_____

Client Actions :

✓ _____
✓ _____
✓ _____
✓ _____
✓ _____
✓ _____

Concerns :   Recommendations :

✓ _____
✓ _____
✓ _____
✓ _____
✓ _____
✓ _____

Overall Comments :

_____
_____
_____
_____

Next Session Talking Points :

✓ _____
✓ _____
✓ _____
✓ _____
✓ _____
✓ _____

Next Session Date : _____   End Time : _____

112

Date : _____ Start time : _____ Session No : _____

Client Name : _____ Topic : _____

Session Talking Points :

✓ _____

✓ _____

✓ _____

✓ _____

Key Points from Previous Session :

✓ _____

✓ _____

✓ _____

✓ _____

Notes : _____

_____

_____

_____

_____

_____

_____

_____

_____

_____

_____

_____

_____

_____

_____

_____

_____

_____

Extra Notes :

Client Actions :

✓

✓

✓

Concerns :

✓

✓

✓

Recommendations :

✓

✓

✓

Overall Comments :

Next Session Talking Points :

✓

✓

✓

Next Session Date : _____   End Time : _____

Date : _____ Start time : _____ Session No : _____

Client Name : _____ Topic : _____

Session Talking Points :

✔ _____

✔ _____

✔ _____

✔ _____

Key Points from Previous Session :

✔ _____

✔ _____

✔ _____

✔ _____

Notes : _____

Extra Notes :

_____
_____
_____
_____
_____
_____
_____

Client Actions :

✓ _____
✓ _____
✓ _____
✓ _____
✓ _____
✓ _____

Concerns :   Recommendations :

✓ _____   ✓ _____
✓ _____   ✓ _____
✓ _____   ✓ _____

Overall Comments :

_____
_____
_____
_____

Next Session Talking Points :

✓ _____
✓ _____
✓ _____
✓ _____
✓ _____
✓ _____

Next Session Date : _____   End Time : _____

Made in the USA
Coppell, TX
11 March 2024

29958886R00070